How Can I Help?

Sher the Polar Bear

Frances Rodgers and Ben Grisdale

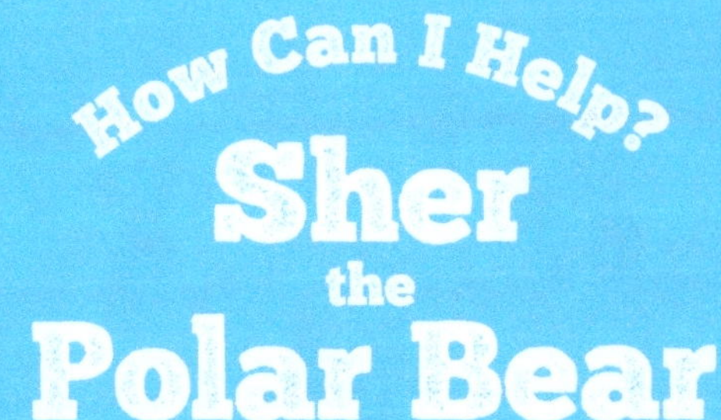

Written and Ilustrated by
Frances Rodgers and *Ben Grisdale*

Editing, design and typesetting by
UK Book Publishing

Editor: *Ruth Lunn*
Designer: *Jason Thompson*

UK BookPublishing.com

First published in Great Britain as a softback original in 2021

Copyright © Frances Rodgers and Ben Grisdale

The moral right of the authors has been asserted.

Typeset in ChunkFive

ISBN: 978-1-8380019-4-0

How Can I Help?

Sher the Polar Bear

Hello, my name is Sher.

I am a polar bear and

I need your help.

I live in snow and ice

in a place called The Arctic,

which is at the top of the world.

The Arctic ice helps to keep
the world's temperature level
by reflecting the heat from
the sun back into space.

HEAT

Our world is getting warmer because

of humans, and each year there is

less snow and ice for me to live on.

The more the snow and ice melt,

the more the sea will rise,

which will cause the land to flood.

The sea has risen 20cm in the past

100 years, and is expected to rise

by another 30cm in the next 30.

2050
TODAY
1920

The fuels that we use every day,
like electricity, gas, oil and petrol,
are a big reason the world is
getting warmer.

Electricity is made by burning
what are known as 'fossil fuels',
such as coal and gas.

CARBON
DIOXIDE
GAS

You can help me by using

less electricity.

LESS
MORE
ELECTRICITY
METER

Please switch off your lights,
televisions and computers when
you are not using them.

Please help me by walking to

school if your journey is short.

Even a short car journey uses

more fuel, which then sends

more fumes into the air.

SCHOOL

SCHOOL

The fumes from cars and lorries

are making the world warm up too.

CARBON DIOXIDE
FUMES
FUMES
NO NEED
TRANSPORT

Another big cause of gas

in the air is cows!

Most cows exist to supply people

with meat, like steaks and burgers.

Cows pump so much, it makes

meat production the 4th biggest

cause of global warming!

FFFt
PUMP
PRRT

You can help me by eating less meat.
If we all stop eating as much meat,
it will reduce the gas that is
making the world warmer.

If everyone can use their cars less,

reduce the electricity they use,

and how much meat they eat,

then between us all,

we can help to slow down or stop

the warming of our world together.

TOO HOT
JUST RIGHT
TOO COLD

Please talk to your family
and friends. You can help me
more by encouraging others
to follow these easy steps.

YOU CAN HELP TOO

Thank you for all of your help.

Now that you know how to help SHER, don't forget to help Dale, Tara and Ryan too!

Available now on AMAZON and other online retailers!

www.ingramcontent.com/pod-product-compliance
Lightning Source LLC
Chambersburg PA
CBHW041053050726
47599CB00018B/2133